Preschool Math

Theme Units for Content-Area Learning

Written by Lily Erlic

Illustrated by Janet Armbrust

Teaching & Learning Company

1204 Buchanan St., P.O. Box 10
Carthage, IL 62321-0010

This book belongs to

Table of Contents

Cover design by Jenny Morgan and Sara King.

Copyright © 2008, Teaching & Learning Company

ISBN 13: 978-1-57310-544-6

ISBN 10: 1-57310-544-9

Printing No. 987654321

Teaching & Learning Company
1204 Buchanan St., P.O. Box 10
Carthage, IL 62321-0010

At the time of publication, every effort was made to insure the accuracy of the information included in this book. However, we cannot guarantee that the agencies and organizations mentioned will continue to operate or to maintain these current locations.

Activities

Simple Patterns

Show children several examples of patterns. Use pictures cut from magazines or actual fruit and vegetables to illustrate simple patterns. Then ask, "What comes next?"

Patterns in Nature

Look for patterns in nature when you go for a walk, on book covers, during story time, on classroom toys—wherever you can find them. Help children see that patterns are all around us. Here are some more ways to find and appreciate patterns:

- Who has a pattern on their clothes?
- Who can draw a pattern on the chalkboard?
- What patterns can you see in the room?
- What patterns can you see at home?

Comparing Patterns

Display two patterns for children to compare. Then ask:

- What is different about these patterns?
- What is the same about these patterns?
Repeat for several pairs of simple patterns.

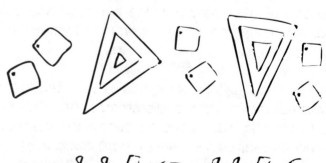

Pattern Fish

By Anne Canevarl Green
Lerner Publishing Group, 2000

Pattern Fish was written by a teacher who wrote this book to use in the classroom. It is an excellent tool for encouraging kids to become aware of patterns, or rhythms. The simple AB pattern is used in the beginning, featuring a fish that is "yellowblack, yellowblack, yellowblack" and the "chompchompmunchmunch" of the sea horse eating seaweed for lunch is an AABB pattern. The amusing illustrations of the various sea creatures, including a smiling octopus moving along with a "stretchspurtglide" plus the rhythmic text make this a very popular book with young learners. Pattern comprehension is not the easiest thing to teach, but this book will help tremendously. Students will love the funny, surprising ending!

Pattern

By Henry Arthur Pluckrose
HarperCollins, 2000

Each page of this book is a vibrant, full-color photograph with a short caption or simple text illustrating an example of patterning. Children are introduced to the concept by using a simple checkerboard layout and eventually move on to an aerial view of rooftops, the border of a carpet, plaid, wallpaper and the petals of a flower. This book is a part of the author's Math Counts series for early learners.

Beep Beep, Vroom Vroom!

By Stuart J. Murphy
HarperCollins, 2000

This lively picture book uses a story from a child's daily world to teach the basic math concept of patterns. Kevin has red, yellow and blue cars that he always lines up in a special way on his shelf. His little sister Molly wants to play, but is told she is too young. Of course, as soon as Kevin leaves the room Molly starts playing with them and every time someone comes in the room she lines up the vehicles in different sequences. At the back there are practical suggestions for adults and kids to find patterns on the pages and to make their own patterns with pebbles, buttons, coins and kitchen utensils. Discussion questions and suggestions for further reading round out this selection, but kids are mostly going to enjoy this book because of its colorful pictures and "vrooming" action.

4

What Comes Next?

Fruit Salad

Cut up some bananas.

Draw what comes next.

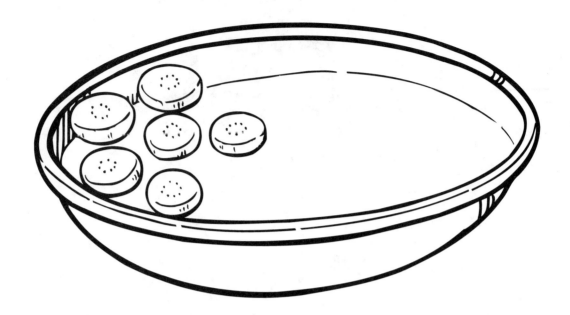

Put them in a bowl.

Copy the banana slice pattern on the other side of the bowl.

2

Add some strawberries,

Draw what comes next.

3

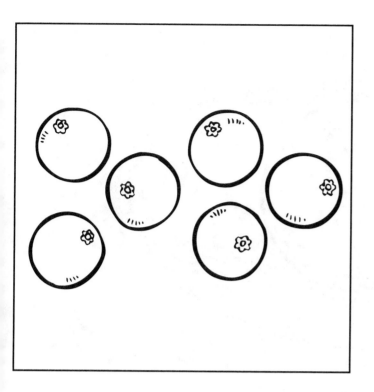

And blueberries too.

Copy the pattern in the box.

4

Add some pineapple,

Finish the pattern.

5

7

And an orange or two.

Draw what comes next.

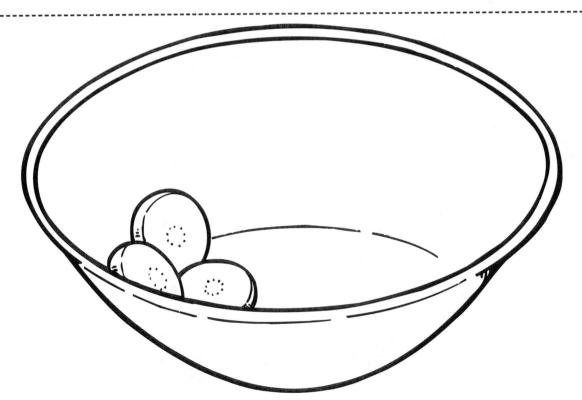

Put them all in the bowl.

Draw the fruits in a pattern in the bowl.

Add pears and apples,

Draw what comes next.

8

And maybe some plums.

Draw 5 plums in a pattern.

9

9

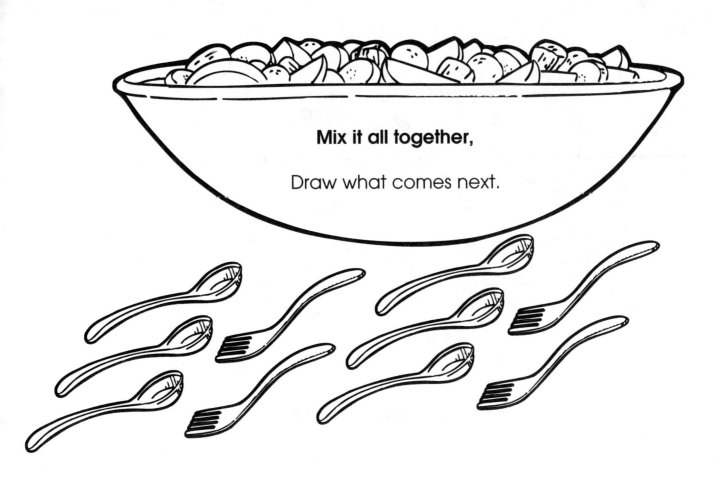

Mix it all together,

Draw what comes next.

12

Have a nice, fruity treat!

13

I Can Make a Pattern

1. Cut out these shapes.
2. Use them to make a pattern.
3. Glue your pattern on a sheet of colored paper.

A Basket Full of Patterns!

1. Cut out the apples and oranges.
2. Place the fruit in the basket to form a pattern.
3. What is your pattern? Explain to the class.

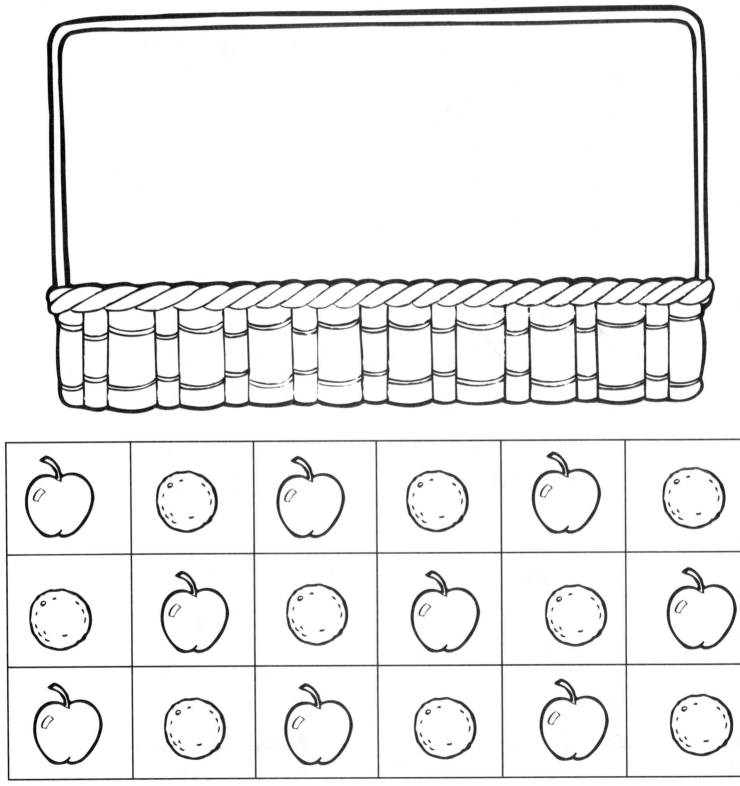

What Comes Next?

Draw the shape that comes next.

1. ☐ ◯ ☐ ◯ ☐ ◯ ___

2. ☐ ☐ ◯ ☐ ☐ ◯ ___

3. ☐ △ ☐ △ ☐ △ ___

4. ☐ ◯ ◯ ☐ ◯ ◯ ___

5. ☐ ☐ ◯ ◯ ☐ ☐ ___

6. ☐ △ ◯ ☐ △ ◯ ___

Fruit Patterns

1. Look at each pattern.
2. Draw the food that comes next on the line.

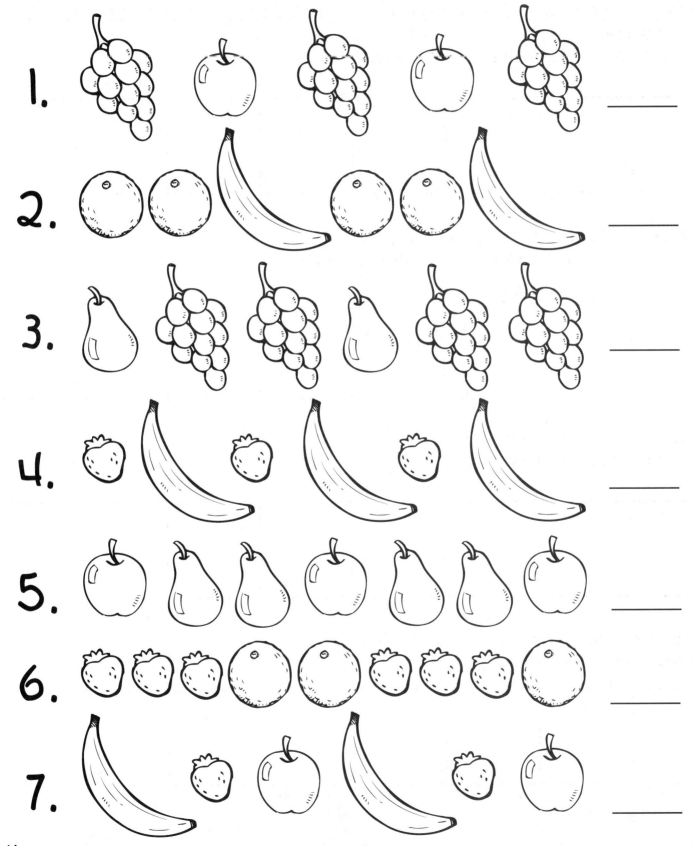

Making Bean Patterns

1. Make a pattern with dried green peas, dried kidney beans and dried navy beans on your desk.
2. Draw or glue your patterns in the squares below.

3. Make a different bean pattern on your desk.
4. Draw or glue that pattern in the squares below.

5. Make another pattern with beans.
6. Draw or glue your new pattern below.

7. Can you make one more bean pattern?
8. Draw or glue the pattern below.

Matching Patterns

1. Find the rows that have the same pattern as the top row.
2. Draw a line through the rows that do not match.

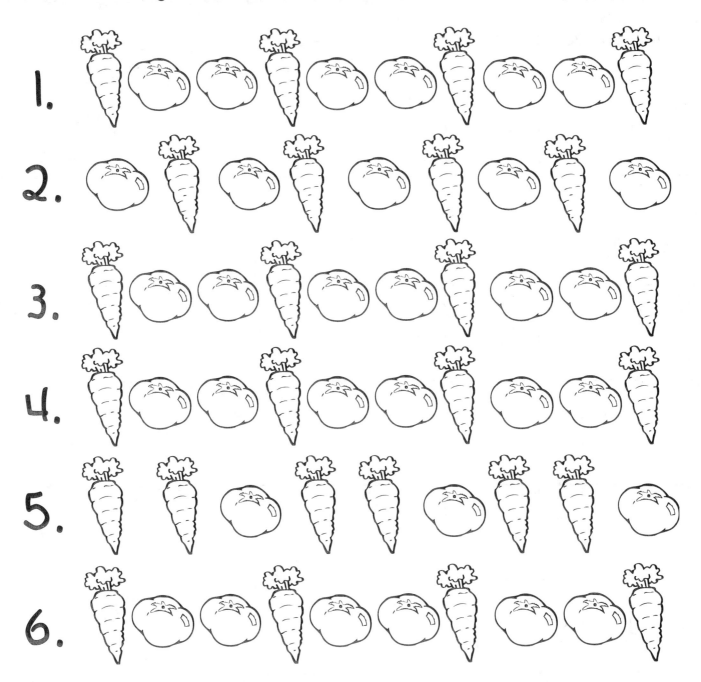

- How many tomatoes are in the top row? _____

- How many tomatoes with stems are in that row? _____

- How many tomatoes with no stems are in that row? _____

16

Name _____

My Patterns Page

Clip Art

Book Cover

My Pattern Book

Name

I Can Make a Pattern!

can make PERFECT PATTERNS!

_____
(Name)

_____
(Teacher)

_____
(Date)

Activities

Simple Sorting

Show children several examples of sorting. Use pictures of food from magazines to practice simple sorting. Then ask, "Why do these belong together?"

Classroom Sorting

Look for objects to sort in the classroom. You could sort crayons by color, books by size or blocks by shape. After sorting, ask children the following questions:

- Can you tell me about the objects in each set?
- How are the sets different?
- How many objects are in each set?
- Are there other ways to sort these objects?

Sorting Pasta

Give each child the basket reproducible from page 22. Have them sort colored pasta by size, shape or color. Then ask:

- How are the objects the same?
- How are the objects different?

Activities Pattern

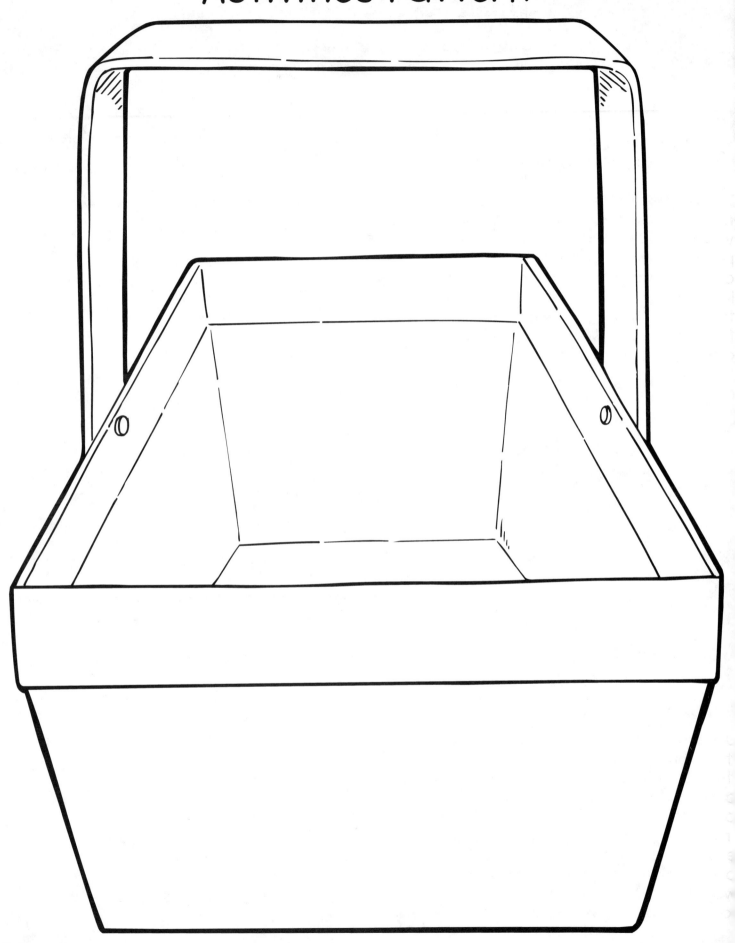

Books

3 Little Firefighters

By Stuart J. Murphy and Emily Rodda
HarperCollins Canada, 2003

This book is a lively introduction to the simple math concept of sorting by attributes. Three young children plan to dress as firefighters for a parade. They start to dress up in their outfits and discover that the buttons are missing. The kids look around and find a bunch of different buttons which they then have to sort so that each firefighter has buttons. The book also includes activities that provide parents or teachers ways to share with their kids the concept of simple math sorting.

Five Creatures

By Emily Jenkins
Farrar, Straus & Giroux, 2001

Three people and two cats are the "five creatures" that are the focus of this lighthearted look at a unique family. They share many traits with one another while maintaining their individuality. This allows the narrator (the little girl in the household) to sort the five by their various commonalities such as hair color, leisure activities and food preferences: "four who like to eat fish. . . two who like to eat mice and only one who likes to eat beets." Around-the-clock glimpses of the day show "one who sings loud late at night" and "one who sings in the morning." Jenkins helps little ones make real-life connections to mathematical concepts such as grouping, Venn diagrams and logical analysis while telling a story that everyone will love.

Sets: Sorting into Groups

By Michele Koomen
Coughlan Publishing 2001

Using a variety of candies, pencils and other things familiar to children, this book introduces the concept of sorting into sets and subsets. It also shows examples from the real world, such as books in a library. A lively cast of children illustrates each point and a hands-on project explores a relevant math idea (piling everybody's shoes on the floor and coming up with ways to sort them). The full-page, full-color photographs will intrigue children of all ages.

Crafts

Food Card Sorting

1. Reproduce the Food Cards on page 25 using pictures of fruit, vegetables, breads and meats.
2. Laminate the cards.
3. Ask the children to sort the cards by size, shape, color or number.

Classroom Food Mural

Give each child a piece of paper. Ask them to draw their favorite healthy foods.

Then cut out the pictures. As a class, sort the foods and glue them on a large piece of paper or bulletin board to create a mural. Label each sorted group. Title the mural *Our Favorite Healthy Foods.*

My Food Cards

Reproduce the Food Cards on page 25. Give each child blank cards made from cardboard. Ask them to draw their own food cards, making sure they create cards they can sort. Practice sorting the cards; then send them home so the children can practice with their families.

Food Cards

FUN with Sorting Food

Some fruits are large and some are small,

Sort the fruits by size. Put an L on each large one and an S on the small ones.

But apples are the best of all!

How can you sort these apples?

2

My favorite meal is mac and cheese.

Circle the kinds of macaroni that go together.

3

May I have a big bowl please?

How can you sort the bowls into two groups?

4

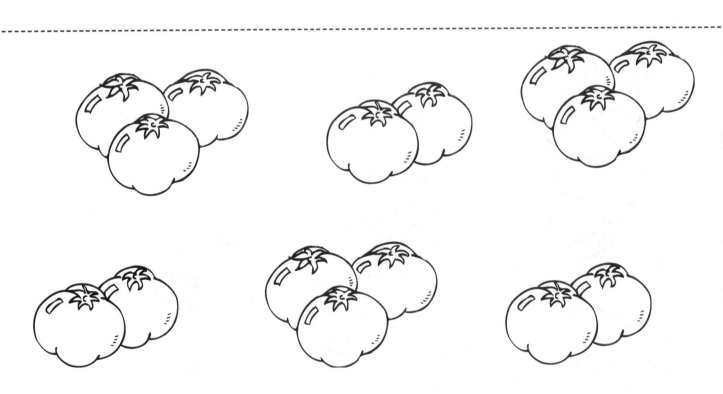

Fresh tomatoes taste so great

Sort the tomatoes into groups.

5

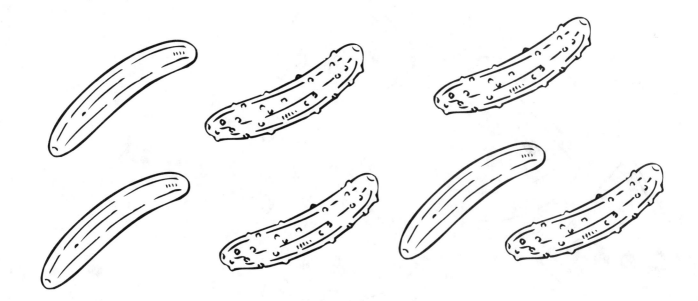

With cucumbers on my plate.

How are the cucumbers different?

6

Bread and butter is a treat

Divide the food into two groups.
Write a 1 or a 2 on each piece to show its group.

7

And watermelon tastes so sweet.

How can you sort the watermelon pieces?

8

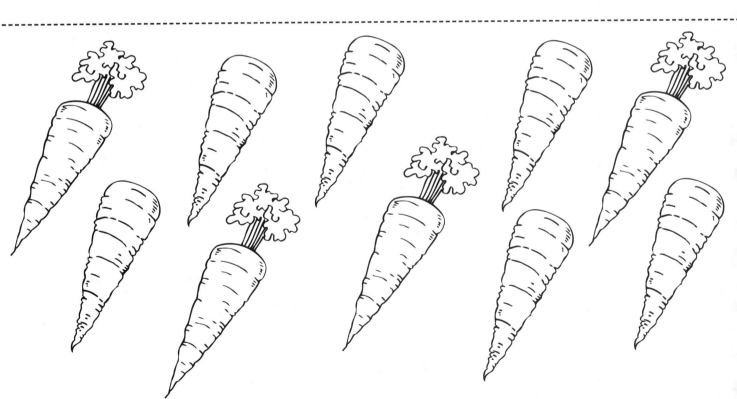

Carrots are so fun to crunch.

Sort the carrots into two groups.

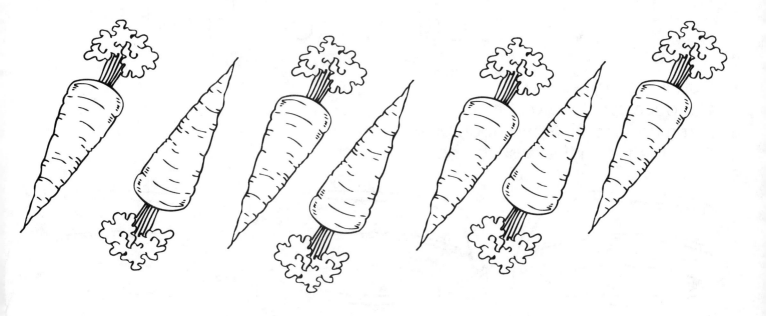

I want some right now to munch!

Number each carrot 1 or 2 to show how you can sort them.

10

Is it lunchtime yet?

11

My Baskets of Fruit

1. Cut along dotted line.
2. Cut out each square of fruit below.
3. Sort matching fruits into each basket.
4. Glue the fruit in the baskets and color each set.

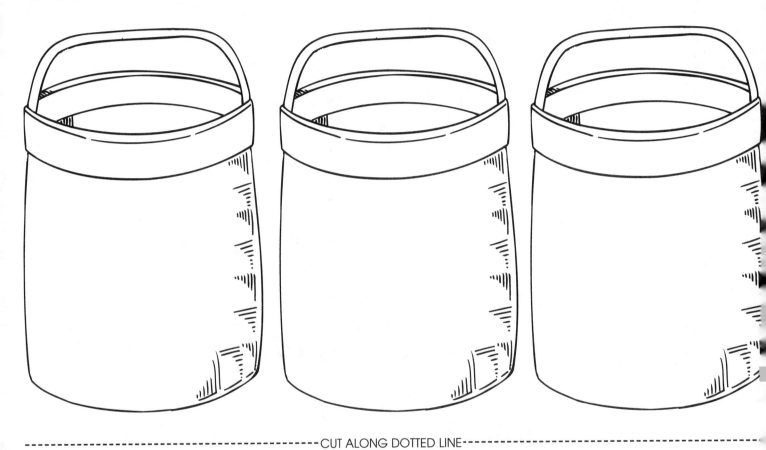

‑‑‑‑‑‑‑‑‑‑‑‑‑‑‑‑‑‑‑‑‑‑‑‑ CUT ALONG DOTTED LINE ‑‑‑‑‑‑‑‑‑‑‑‑‑‑‑‑‑‑‑‑‑‑‑‑

Sorting Beans

1. Divide the class into groups.
2. Provide each group with a basket of dried beans in various shapes and colors.
3. Ask the groups to sort the beans.
4. Ask: How are the beans the same? How are they different?
5. Groups can use the sorting circle below to help them.

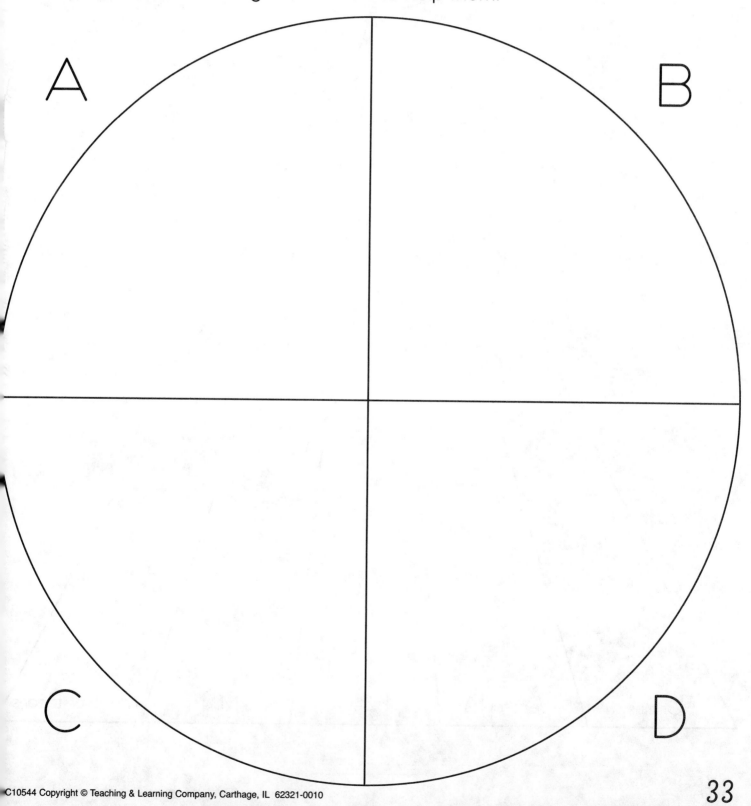

The Food Pyramid

1. Talk about each of the food groups in the pyramid.
2. Draw two foods that go in each category.
3. Discuss how the food pyramid helps us sort foods.

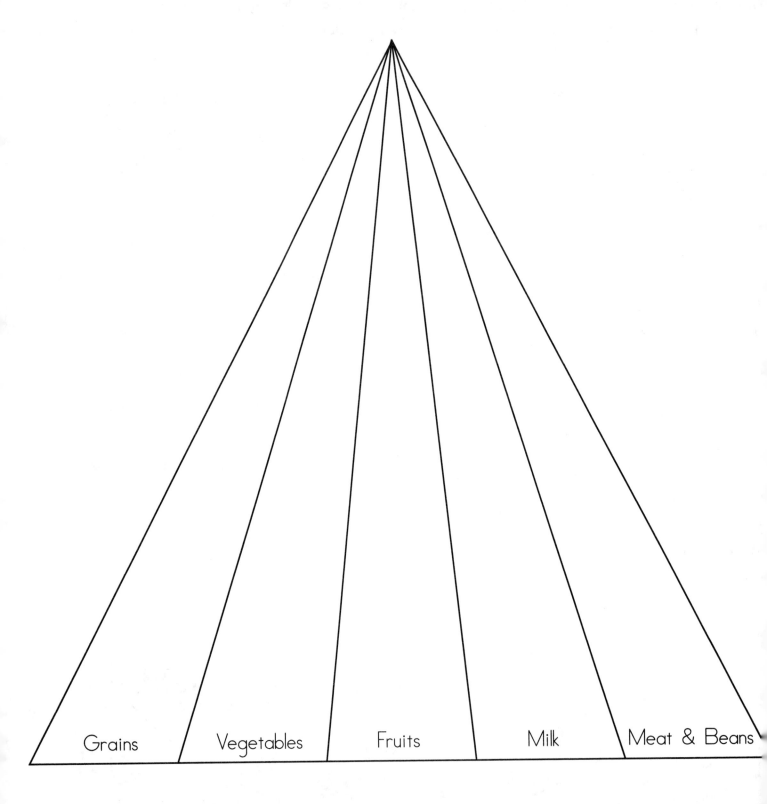

Grains   Vegetables   Fruits   Milk   Meat & Beans

Name _____

My Sorting Page

My Sorting Book

_____
Name

I Can Sort!

_____
(Name)

is a SUPER SORTER!

_____
(Teacher)

_____
(Date)

38

Activities

Identify Numbers 1-10

Copy and cut out the Numbers cards on page 40 and share with the children. Help them to identify the numbers 1-10. Demonstrate each number using dried beans or pasta.

Cookie Count

Copy and cut out the Cookies reproducible on page 41. As a group, count the chocolate chips and put the cookies in order from one to 10.

Then ask:
* Which cookie has seven chocolate chips?
* Which one has five chocolate chips?
* Which cookie has the most chocolate chips?
* Which cookie has the least amount of chocolate chips?

Simple Addition

Copy and cut out the Cookies reproducible on page 41 to help children practice simple addition.

* Take two cookies and add the chocolate chips. Repeat with several pairs of cookies.
* Give each child a piece of paper and encourage children to draw their own chocolate chip cookies. Then have them write the number of chocolate chips by each cookie.

Number Cards

Cookies

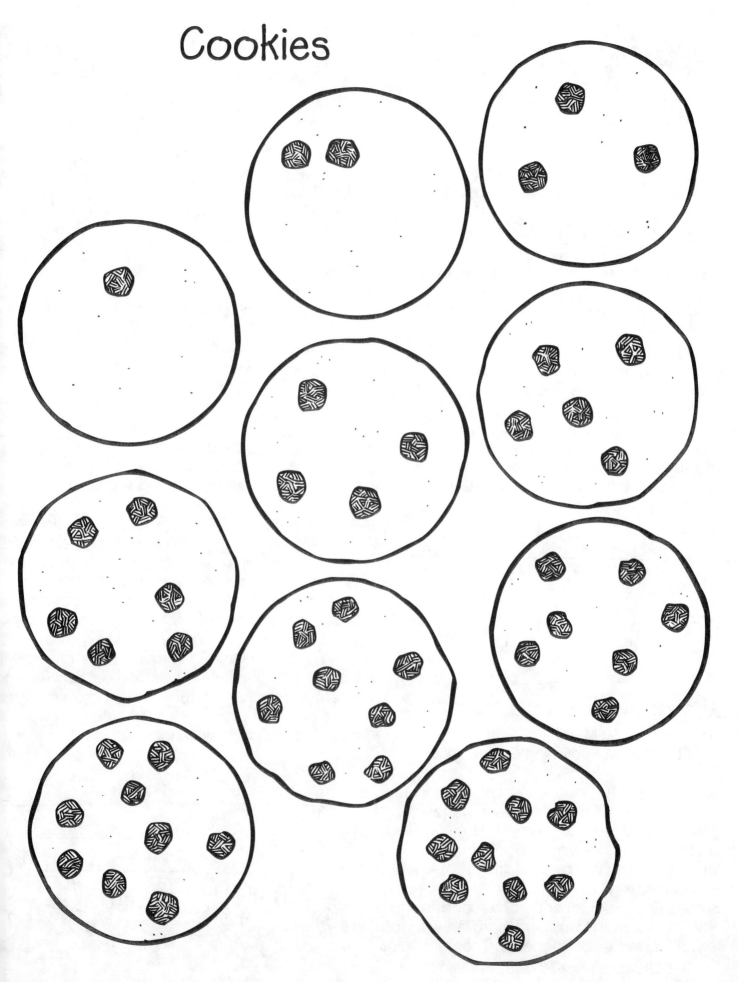

Books

Click, Clack, Splish, Splash: A Counting Adventure
By Doreen Cronin
Simon & Schuster Children's Publishing, 2006

As the farmer naps on the couch near his fish tank ("1 farmer sleeping"), Duck ("2 feet creeping") and the other barnyard animals sneak into the house on a well-intentioned but mischievous mission that involves "3 buckets piled high" outside the window and "4 chickens standing by." This numerical adventure for ages 2-5 offers a comical introduction to numbers one through 10 and is the counting companion to the very popular *Click, Clack, Quackity Quack: An Alphabetical Adventure.*

Chicka Chicka 1, 2, 3
By Bill Martin, Jr.,
Michael Sampson and Lois Ehlert
Simon & Schuster Children's Publishing, 2004

This spectacular follow-up to the classic bestseller *Chicka Chicka Boom Boom* is perfect for any child learning to count and in the process of learning their numbers. In this book numbers take over an apple tree and work on climbing to the top ("1 told 2 and 2 told 3, I'll race you to the top of the apple tree"). As the numbers climb one by one, a worried zero wonders if there will be room for him. In the meantime, bumblebees threaten to spoil the fun and a hero emerges. This book is guaranteed to entertain as well as reinforce counting skills and digit identification.

Ten Little Ladybugs
By Melanie Gerth
Dalmatian Publishing Group, 2006

One by one, 10 touchable bugs disappear. Where did they all go? Little ones will love finding out as they feel their way through the colorful pages of this innovative book. The cute little critters provide a hands-on learning experience and the rhyming text reinforces the concept of counting. This magical countdown adds up to a whole lot of fun! This colorful board book is both interactive and educational and features plastic ladybugs embedded into the pages.

42

Crafts

Number Cards

1. Reproduce the Number Cards on page 44.
2. Have each child color a set of cards.
3. Have children cut cards apart.
4. Send cards home so children can practice their numbers with their families.

Cookie Count

1. Reproduce the Cookies on page 45.
2. Have children color their cookies.
3. Instruct children to draw one chocolate chip on one of their cookies.
4. Have children turn the cookie over and write the number 1.
5. Repeat steps 3 and 4 for the numbers 2-10 on the remaining cookies.

Number Cards

1	2
3	4
5	6
7	8
9	10

44

Cookies

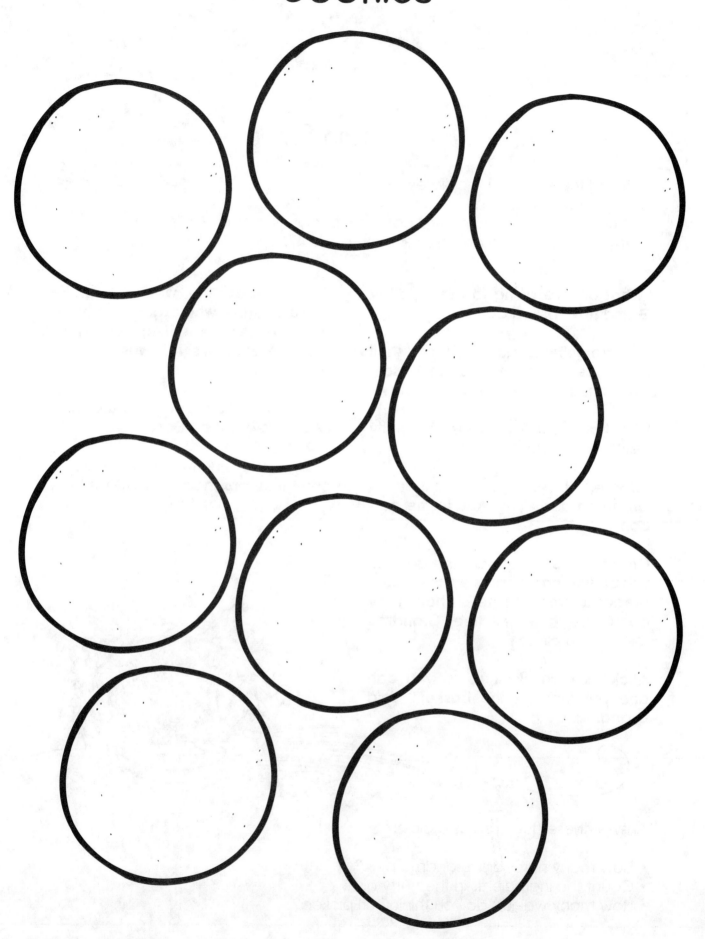

Short Story

A Counting Story

1. Read the story to the children.
2. Use a felt board to help count the ingredients.
3. Create felt pieces using the patterns for chives, parsley, rosemary, oregano, thyme, walnut tree and a squirrel on page 47.

"What are we going to make today Grandma?" asked Carl.

"We are going to make a nutty dish. It has herbs, rice and walnuts in it," said Grandma as she washed her hands.

"What do we need to make the nutty dish?" asked Carl.

"Come, I'll show you," answered Grandma as they walked to the garden.

Grandma cut herbs from the garden. She picked chives, parsley, rosemary, oregano and thyme. When they came to the walnut tree, Grandma told Carl to climb it.

"Pick as many walnuts as you can and put them in the basket," said Grandma.

Carl climbed the walnut tree. He could see the whole garden from it. Then, he felt something tickling his hand. A squirrel's tail was brushing against him.

"Do I have enough walnuts now, Grandma?" asked Carl.

"Yes, now let's go to the kitchen so we can make our meal!" said Grandma.

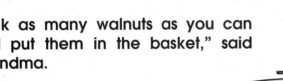

Answer these questions as a class:

- How many herbs did Grandma pick?
- Count the ingredients in the nutty dish.
- How many walnuts do you think Carl picked?

Short Story Patterns

How Many Treats?

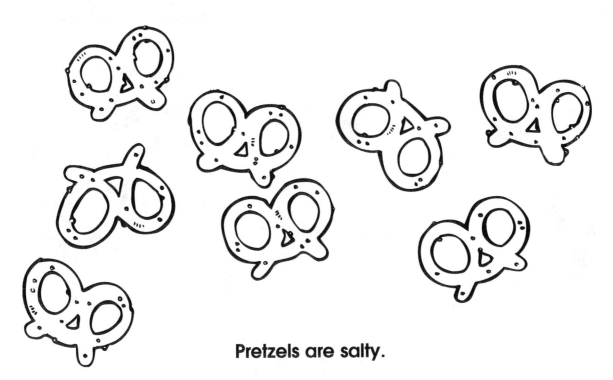

Pretzels are salty.

Count the pretzels.

1

Peanuts go crunch!

Add enough peanuts to make 10 in the bowl.

2

Popcorn is fun.

How many pieces of popcorn do you see?

3

49

I like grapes a bunch.

Count the grapes forwards and backwards.

4

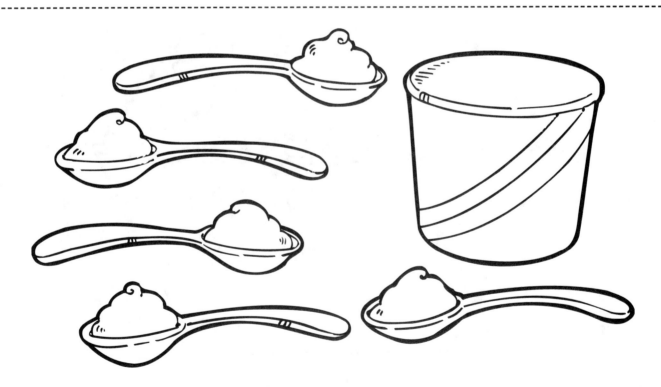

Yogurt is smooth.

How many spoonfuls do you want?

5

Peanut butter is too.

Count the jars of peanut butter.

6

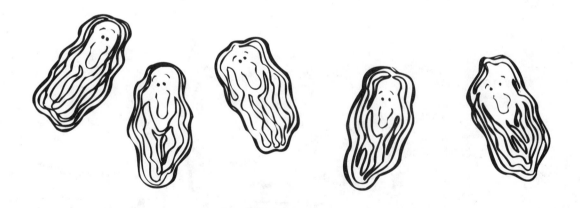

Raisins are wrinkly,

Count the raisins backwards, starting with 5.

7

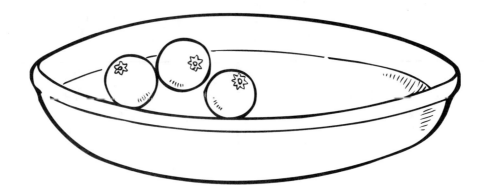

Blueberries are blue.

Draw three more blueberries in the dish.

8

Ice cream is my favorite.

Count the dips on the ice cream cone.

9

It's cold in my tummy.

Write a 1 on the boy's shirt.

10

But all of these treats taste really yummy!

11

Blueberry Pancakes

1. Count the blueberries on each pancake.
2. Write the correct number on the line under the pancake.

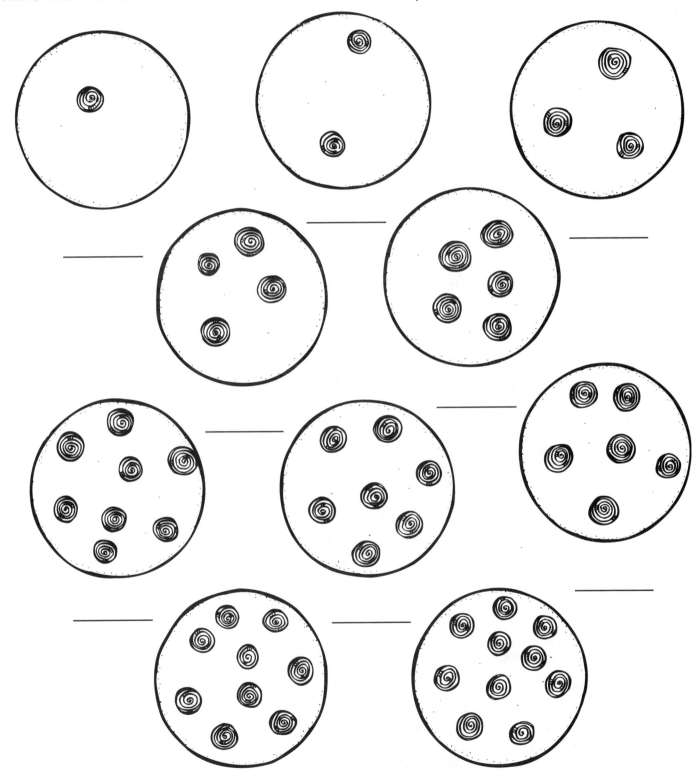

Counting Walnuts

1. How many walnuts are in the basket? _____

2. How many walnuts are in the basket? _____

3. How many walnuts are in the basket? _____

4. How many walnuts are in the basket? _____

Seed Countdown

1. Count the seeds backwards from 10 - 1.
2. Glue or draw the seeds in the chart by each number.

10										
9									
8								
7							
6					
5				
4			
3		
2	
1

56

Name _____

My Numbers Page

1 2 3 4
10   5
9 8 7 6

Book Cover

My Numbers Book

Name

Numbers Are Neat!

(Name)

knows NUMBERS 1-10!

(Date)

(Teacher)

Activities

Tools for Measuring

Show children a ruler, a yardstick and a measuring tape. Talk about what you would use these to measure. Talk about the concepts of big/small and tall/short. Then ask:

• What should we use to measure the height of the chair?
• Is the table taller or shorter than the chair?

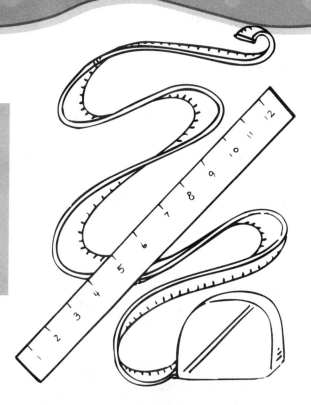

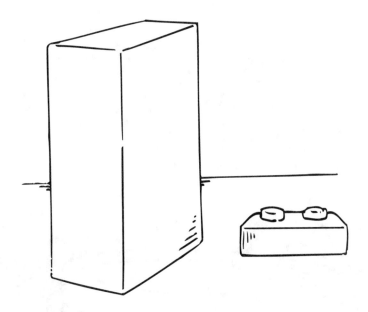

Bigger vs. Smaller

Gather several common classroom items. Hold them up in pairs and have children identify which is bigger or smaller.

Heavy vs. Light

Show children a scale. Discuss the concept of weight as well as heavy and light. Using apples and oranges, ask:

• Is the apple heavier than an orange?
• Are two apples heavier than one apple?
• Are three oranges heavier than one apple?
• Is the table taller or shorter than the chair?

Practice Measuring Activity

1. Practice measuring with measuring spoons and cups.
2. Measure water into a bowl.

- Measure 1 teaspoon of water into a bowl.

- Measure 2 teaspoons of water into a bowl.

- Measure 3 teaspoons of water into a bowl.

- Measure 1 tablespoon of water into a bowl.

- Measure 1 cup of water into a bowl.

- Measure 2 cups of water into a bowl.

- Measure 3 cups of water into a bowl.

Funnel Fun Activity

1. As a class, look at an empty bottle and guess how many cups would fill it.
2. Pour one cup at a time through a funnel.
3. Answer the questions below.

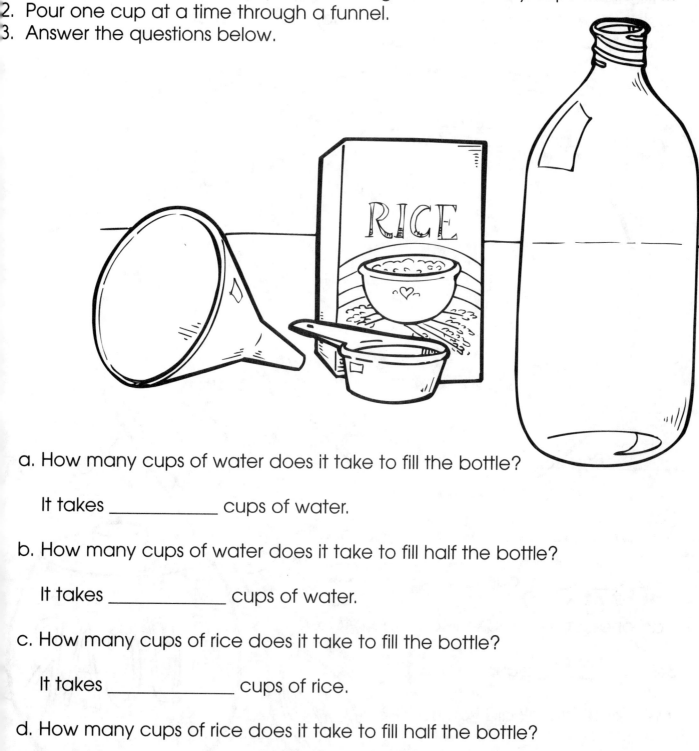

a. How many cups of water does it take to fill the bottle?

   It takes _____ cups of water.

b. How many cups of water does it take to fill half the bottle?

   It takes _____ cups of water.

c. How many cups of rice does it take to fill the bottle?

   It takes _____ cups of rice.

d. How many cups of rice does it take to fill half the bottle?

   It takes _____ cups of rice.

e. Does it take more cups of water or more cups of rice to fill the bottle?

   _____

Making Lemonade Activity

1. Divide the class into groups.
2. Ask each group to measure one cup of sugar into a pitcher.
3. Then they should add one cup of water and stir with a big spoon.

a. Add two more cups of water to your pitcher.

   1 + 2 = _____ cups

b. Add one cup of lemon juice to the pitcher.

   3 + 1 = _____ cups

c. What kind of drink did you make?

   We made _____.

d. Pour the lemonade from the pitcher into small paper cups. How many cups d
   you make?

   We made _____ cups of lemonade.

64

Ravioli Feast Activity

1. As a class, count the ravioli.
2. Measure one ravioli.
3. Cook the ravioli and then measure it again.

a. How many ravioli shapes are there? _____

b. Measure the ravioli with your ruler.

   How big is the side of the square? _____

c. Measure the ravioli after it is cooked.

   Now what is the size of the ravioli? _____

d. Does the ravioli get bigger or smaller when it is cooked? _____

Books

Inch by Inch
By Leo Leonni
HarperCollins Publishers, 1995

This Caldecott Honor Book is the story of a smart inchworm that gets out of harm's way by doing what he does best—measure. When he first encounters a robin that is ready to gobble him up, he uses his wit to measure the bird who is so impressed by the inchworm that he takes him to his friends to do measurements. This humorous tale is a simple book that introduces the concept of measurement including the measurement of music.

Counting on Frank
By Rod Clement
Houghton Mifflin, 1994

This book contains wonderful illustrations of c boy and his rambunctious dog Frank. The boy likes to ask questions about ordinary things like ball-point pens, peas and his dog. "What if drew with this pen until it ran out, how long would the line be?" The boy uses Frank as a uni of measure while calculating fascinating and interesting facts about peas, humpback whales his father and the bathtub. "What if I ran thi bath until the room filled up with water, how long would it take?" Counting on Frank inspires read ers to think about measurement and laugh a the same time. It is a wonderful book full of inter esting facts about numbers, calculation and c dog named Frank!

Size: Many Ways to Measure
By Michele Koomen
Coughlan Publishing, 2001

Using a variety of animals and kids, this text explores the idea of size including length, volume and measuring in nonstandard and standard units. An intriguing cast of children illustrates each point and a hands-on project explores a relevant math idea such as measuring a foot. The book includes a pronunciation glossary, a list of other books related to size and measuring, Internet sources and an index.

66

How Big? How Small?

Sometimes big and small is easy to see.

Which is bigger—the tree or the apple?

1

Sometimes we have to look closely.

Number the smallest apple 1 and the largest one 6.

2

When we aren't sure of something's size,

Color the small pie red and the large pie green.

3

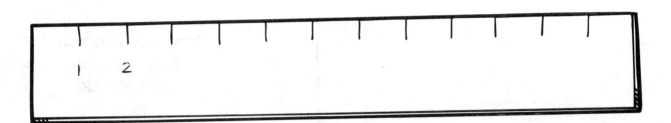

We can use a ruler, not just our eyes.

Finish the numbers on the ruler to show inches.

4

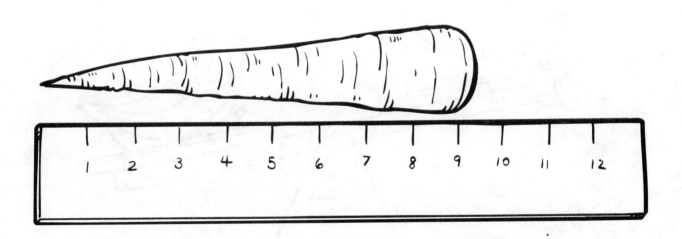

A ruler is for how long or wide.

How many inches long is the carrot?

5

You can measure down or from side to side.

How many inches tall is the box?

6

Find out if something is heavy or light;

Which bunch of bananas is heavier?

7

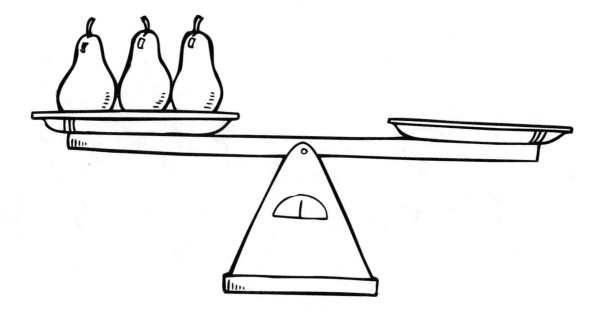

Use a scale and get it right.

Draw on the right side of the scale the number of pears to balance it.

8

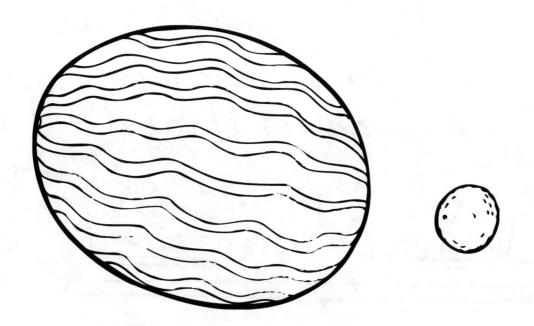

Sometimes it's easy to look and guess

Which do you think weighs more?

9

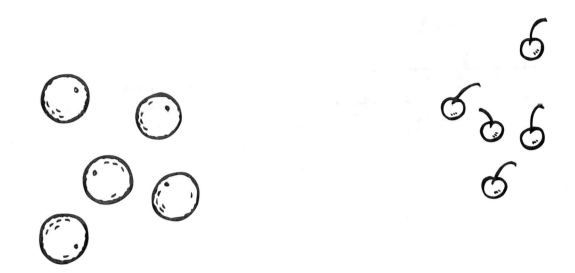

To see if the weight is more or less.

Which group of fruit would weigh less.

10

It's fun to measure all kinds of things!

11

Name _____

Long or Short?

Circle the longest piece of spaghetti in each group.

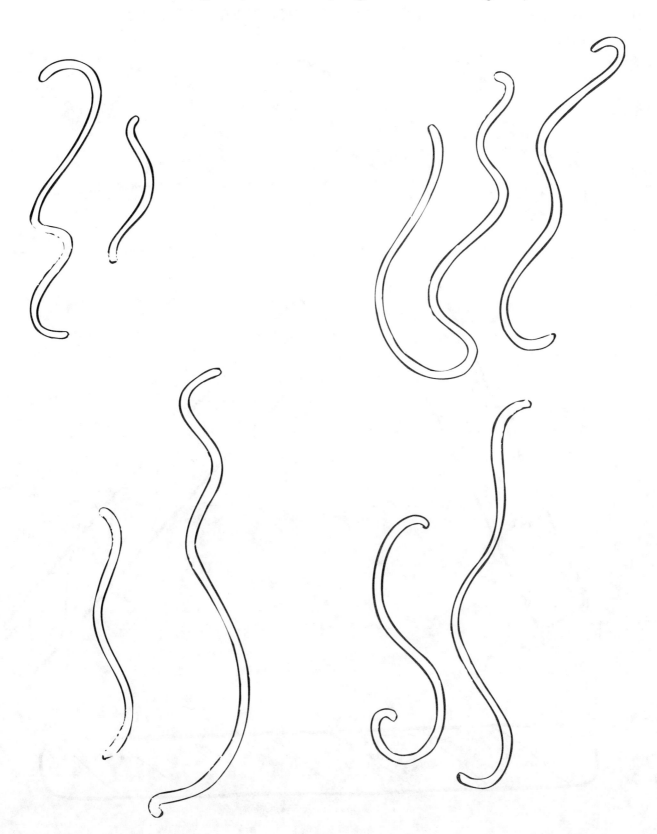

Using a Ruler

1. Use a ruler to measure each of the crackers.
2. Write down the number of inches across (long) each cracker is.

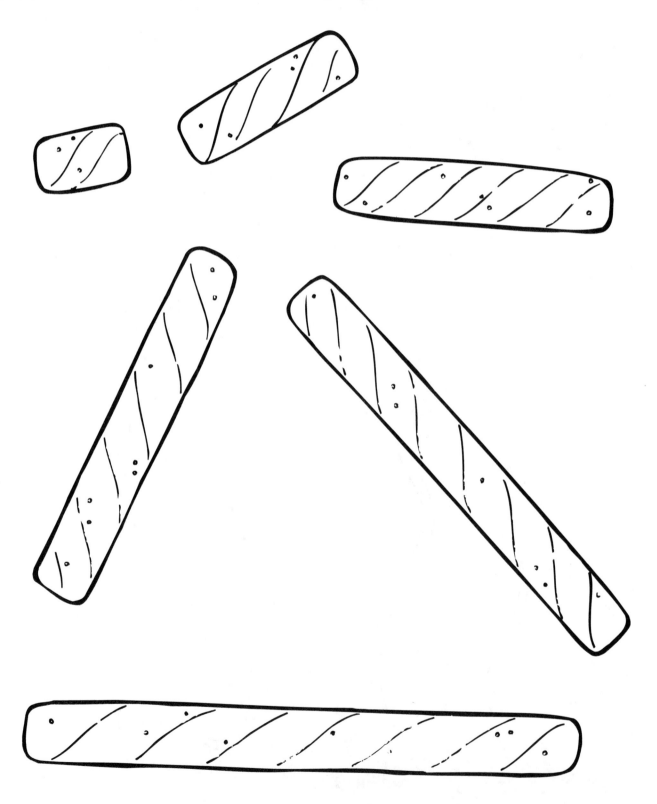

Name _____

Book Cover

My
Measuring
Book

Name _____

I Can Measure!

(Name)

is a MAGNIFICENT MEASURER!

(Teacher)

(Date)

Activities

Shape Walk

Take a shape walk around the classroom. Ask the children to identify as many shapes as they can. Then ask:

- Did you see any squares? Where?
- Where are the circles in the room?
- What other shapes did you see?

Drawing Shapes

Draw various shapes on the board. Ask the children to draw the same shapes on a piece of paper. Or provide the "Tracing Shapes" reproducible on page 89. Encourage children to:

- Draw (or trace) a square.
- Draw (or trace) a circle.
- Draw (or trace) a rectangle.
- Draw (or trace) a triangle.

Build with Shapes

Provide the children with three-dimensional shape blocks and encourage them to build. Ask:

- What did you make?
- What shapes did you use?

Books

The Greedy Triangle

By Marilyn Burns
Scholastic, 1995

In this lively introduction to shapes and polygons, a bored triangle is turned into a quadrilateral after a visit to the shapeshifter. Delighted with the results and his new career opportunities as a TV screen and a picture frame, he asks for more and more changes and ends up with so many lines and angles he doesn't know which way is up. Finally an accident teaches him a lesson and all is well. This informative adventure is a great way to teach basic shapes and includes a special teaching section.

Mouse Shapes

By Ellen Soll Walsh
Harcourt Children's Books, 2007

When three little mice run from a cat, they find a cluster of brightly colored squares, triangles, rectangles, circles, ovals and diamonds where they hide until he leaves. Soon they are moving the shapes about to create pictures including a house, a wagon and even a cat. This visually appealing book features a simple, elegant page design which aids the author in accomplishing her purpose of teaching shapes by combining text and illustration. A great follow-up to the story would be providing cutout colored paper shapes for children to play with and create their own objects and pictures.

Brown Rabbit's Shape Book

By Alan Baker
Kingfisher, 1999

This is a beautiful concept book featuring a very likable character. There are bright colors along with a clever story in which the rabbit hero finds packages inside packages and words that are fun to say like "Whoosh" and "Curly-wurly." Along the way, kids will see examples of a rectangle, an oval, a circle, a square, as well as a tube and other interesting shapes. The text bright colors and an adorable soft-looking bunny makes this book a winner with everyone!

80

A Math Sandwich

Begin with bread.

Which shape would you like?

1

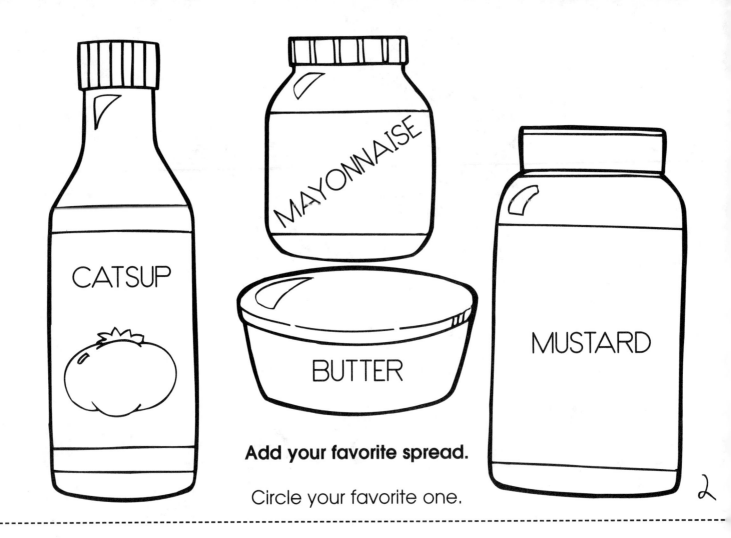

CATSUP

MAYONNAISE

BUTTER

MUSTARD

Add your favorite spread.

Circle your favorite one.

2

Ham or chicken, one slice,

What shape are they?

3

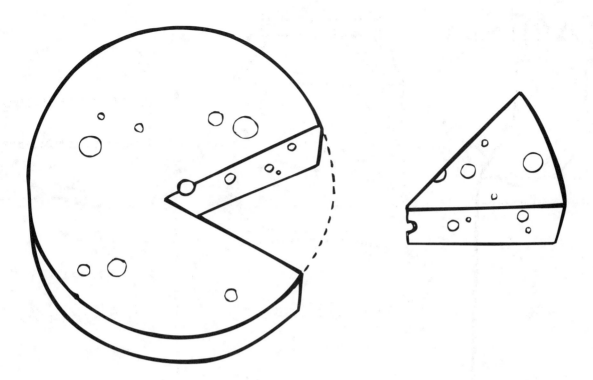

And some cheese would be nice.

What shape is the cheese? What shape is the cut-out piece?

4

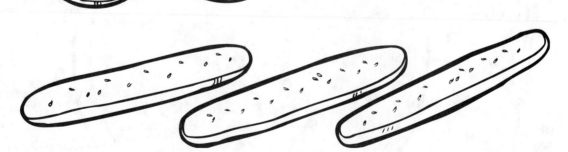

Add pickles for fun,

Which shape do you want? How many?

5

83

And some lettuce (or none).

Draw two more lettuce pieces in different shapes.

6

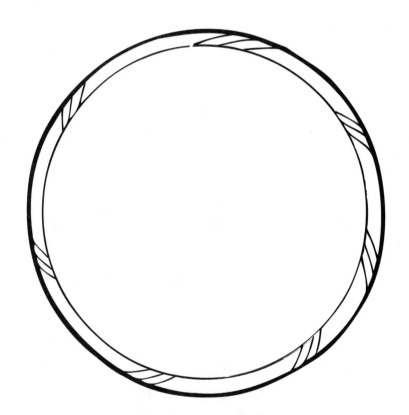

Put it on a plate,

7

Draw your sandwich on the plate.

But don't eat it yet. Wait!

What shape is the sign?

8

- -

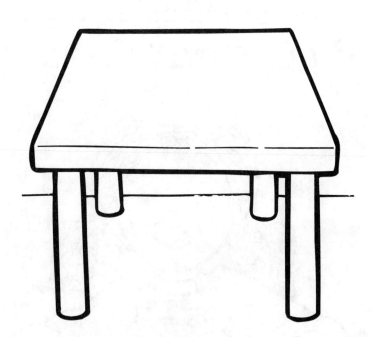

Sit down at the table.

Draw your round plate on the square table.

9

Be neat, if you're able.

Draw a rectangle-shaped napkin next to your plate.

10

Time to eat your math sandwich. YUM!

11

Where Are the Shapes?

1. Color the circles red.
2. Color the squares blue.
3. Color the rectangles yellow.
4. Color the triangles green.
5. Then answer the questions below.

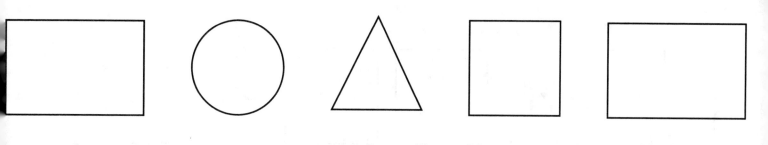

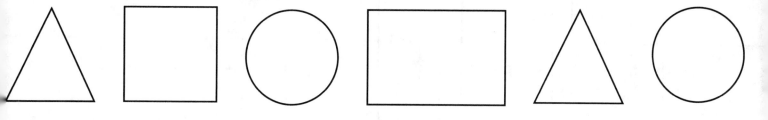

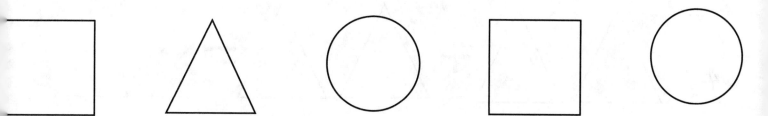

Count the shapes.

- There are _____ circles.
- There are _____ squares.

  There are _____ rectangles.
- There are _____ triangles.

How Many Shapes?

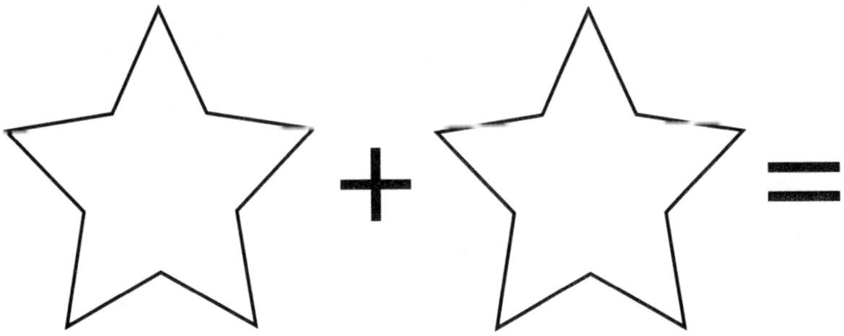

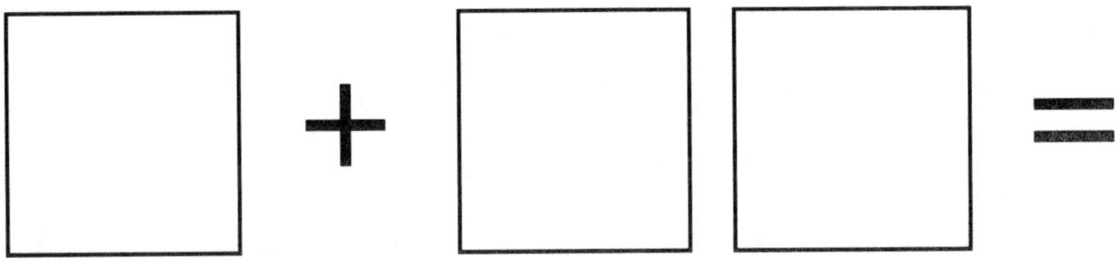

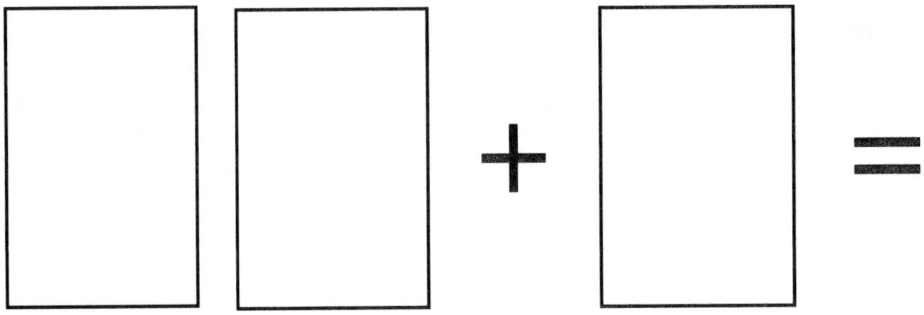

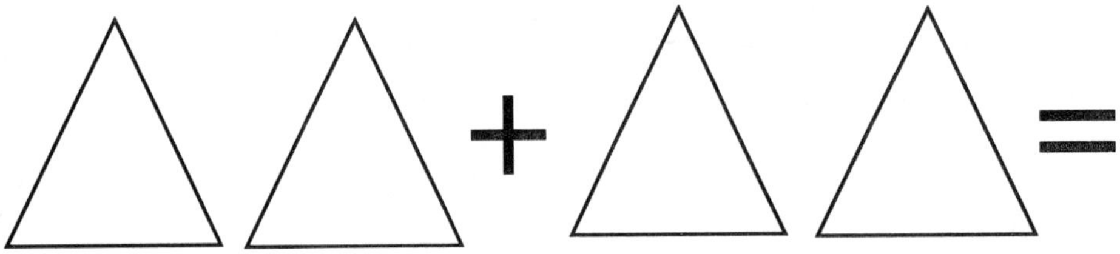

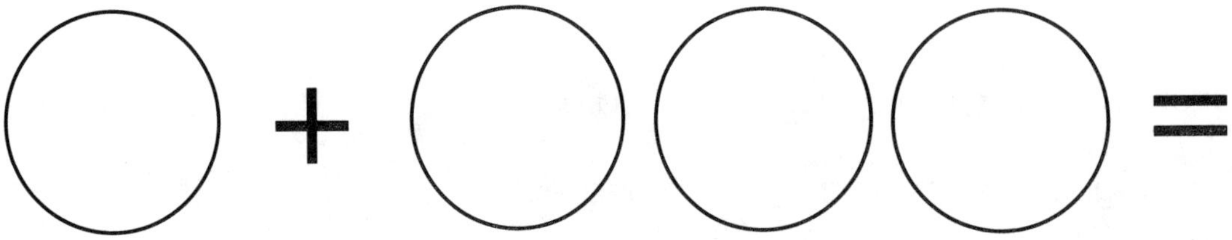

1. ☆ + ☆ = _____

2. ▢ + ▢ ▢ = _____

3. ▯ ▯ + ▯ = _____

4. △ △ + △ △ = _____

5. ◯ + ◯ ◯ ◯ = _____

Tracing Shapes

1. Trace each shape.
2. Color the triangle purple.
3. Color the square orange.
4. Color the circle green.
5. Color the rectangle blue.

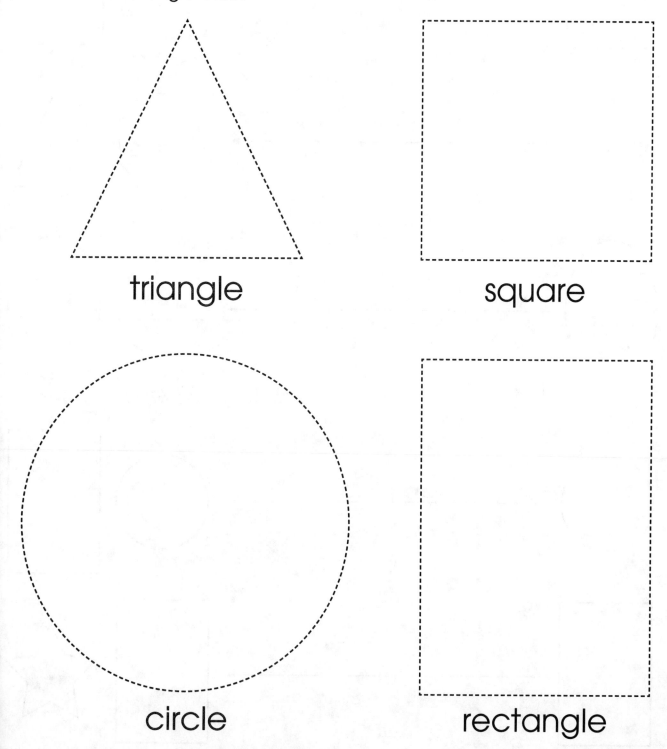

triangle

square

circle

rectangle

Name _____

Match the Shape

1. Color the shapes.
2. Then circle the shape that matches.

1.  ⟶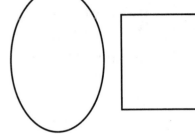

2.  ⟶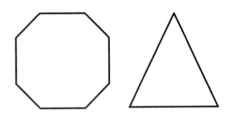

3. 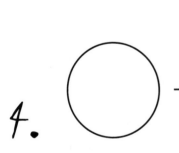 ⟶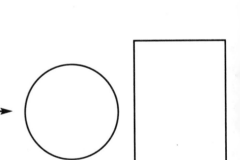

4.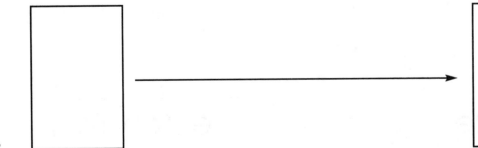

5.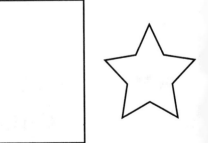

90

Shape Salad

1. Cut apart the shape squares below.
2. Color the shapes.
3. Create a shape salad in the bowl.

-------- CUT ALONG DOTTED LINE --------

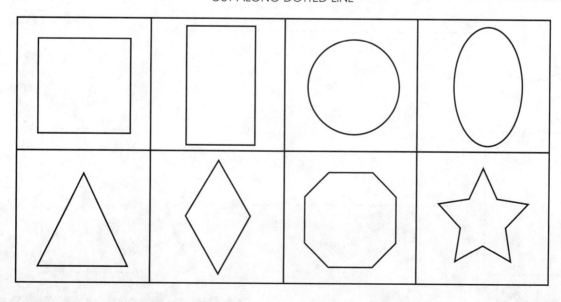

Pasta Shapes

1. Trace lasagna and ravioli.
2. Color the pasta shapes.

Lasagna

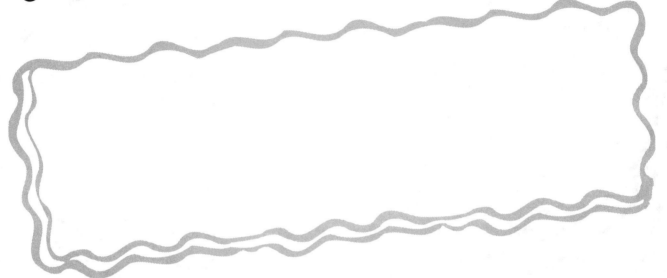

Rectangle

Ravioli

Square

Name _____

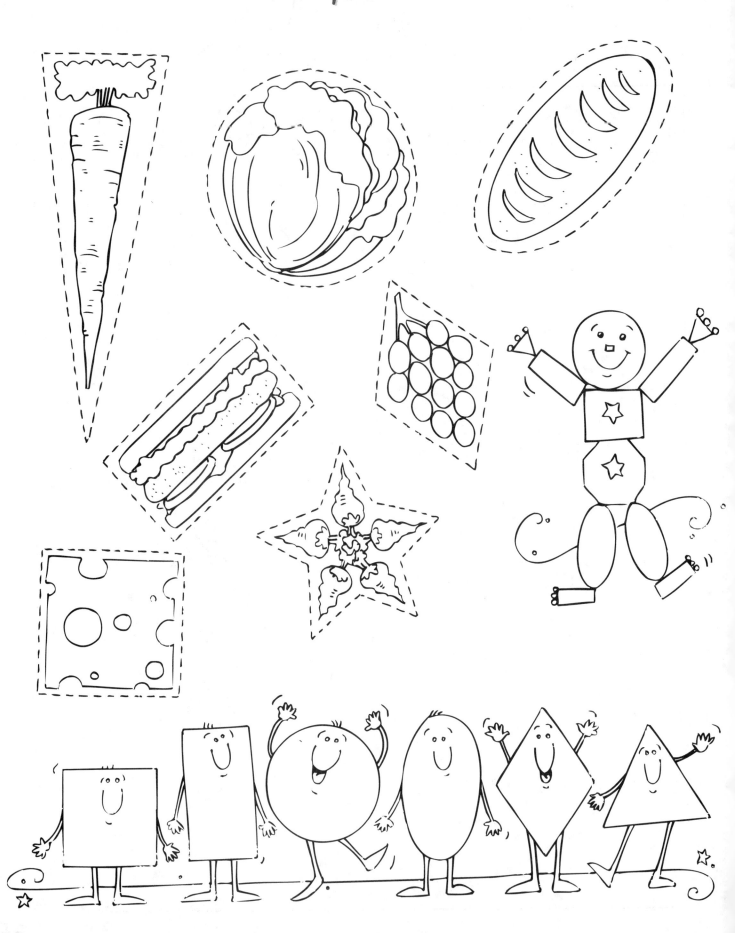

Book Cover

My
Shapes
Book

_____
Name

My
I Know
Shapes!

_____
(Name)

is SUPER with SHAPES!

_____
(Teacher)

_____
(Date)